We Live As Christ

DENNIS F. KINLAW

Edited by John N. Oswalt

FRANCIS ASBURY PRESS
of Evangel Publishing House
Nappanee, Indiana 46550

Toll-Free Order Line: (800) 253-9315 (7:30 a.m.–4:30 p.m. EST)
Internet Website: www.evangelpublishing.com

Cover design by Ted Ferguson
Index by Joseph D. Allison

ISBN 1-928915-23-X
LCCN 2001091064

Printed in the United States of America
9 8 7 6 5 4 3 2 1 / 10 09 08 07 06 05 04 03 02 01

Kenneth Wyatt

3-16-03

Table of Contents

Preface

This book contains a series of lectures presented at the 1999 International Theological Consultation held at Asbury Theological Seminary under the sponsorship of OMS International. The Consultation gathered 81 professors and academic administrators from around the globe, with the stated purpose "to review our historic Wesleyan theological distinctive, to facilitate communication and networking between schools, and to provide a foundation for theological education in the twenty-first century."

I was privileged to share daily platform duties at the Consultation with Dr. Sam Kamaleson, Vice President at Large for World Vision International, and Dr. Manfred Kohl, Vice President for International Development of the Overseas Council. These distinguished Christian leaders and other speakers brought us a series of challenging, visionary presentations.

I would have been glad to attend the Consultation simply to hear what the others had to say, but it was my joyful task to bring these lectures to the assembly as well.

Serving on the board of OMS International during the past thirty years, I have seen the Lord bless this organization with open doors to mission outreach around the world. The Consultation was one of those doors. My friends at OMS International have kindly chosen to publish the lectures in book form, and I am delighted to give this project my support.

My intention in these lectures was to speak simply and informally, so that the ideas could be translated clearly into the various cultural contexts represented by the group. The lectures were not designed to be a comprehensive or fully articulated prospectus for theological education. Given the time constraints of the conference, I could only paint in broad strokes an outline of the task ahead of us. Moreover, I intended to be inspirational rather than didactic in my approach. I hoped to challenge the participants to renew their commitment to Christ, as they undertake their work as educators and missionaries in an often hostile world.

The lectures have been slightly abridged to remove some personal references to OMS staff members and delegates to the Consultation which may not be meaningful to the readers of this book. However, the theological and inspirational substance has been preserved.*

I believe that the Consultation was an important step toward realizing the future of Christian missions and Christian theological education. May this book make another modest contribution to that effort.

> Dennis F. Kinlaw
> Wilmore, Kentucky

---

*NOTE: I have not attempted to use inclusive language for the sake of simplicity. However, I recognize that Scripture passages about Christians apply to women as well as men. So I ask the reader's indulgence when I am using masculine pronouns to refer to Christians in general.

After Jesus said this, he looked toward heaven and prayed:

"Father, the time has come. Glorify your Son, that your Son may glorify you. For you granted him authority over all people that he might give eternal life to all those you have given him. Now this is eternal life: that they may know you, the only true God, and Jesus Christ, whom you have sent. I have brought you glory on earth by completing the work you gave me to do. And now, Father, glorify me in your presence with the glory I had with you before the world began."

—John 17:1-5

1. What God Has Promised Us

WE STAND at an unusual moment in history. There never has been a day quite like this. We could not have convened a conference of evangelical leaders like this fifteen years ago. But the world has changed, so here we are. I have lived to see a day when theoretically not a single person in the world lives beyond the reach of the Gospel message. We have the means to reach everyone for Christ.

I wonder what Charles Cowman[1] would have done if he lived in a day like this, given the passion that burned in his soul and in the souls of those around him, like Juji Nakada. We have the means to share Christ with others which they did not have a century ago.

You and I are here because of a tremendous explosion of Christian evangelism across the face of the world at the end of the nineteenth century. That explosion occurred without the political freedom, the communications technology, or the financial means that we have today. Given these wonderful new possibilities, I ask you: *Is God interested at this moment in doing something very unique in this world?* If so, a group like this could be a crucial part of what He does.

I come to these sessions as an American. This means I come with all the limitations of being an American, and I must speak out of an American's knowledge and experience. You will have to translate my comments for your own context. I want to say some things about the United States which may sound negative, but let me confess that I have been

---

[1]Charles Cowman was an American missionary to Japan in the 1920s and co-founder of the Oriental Missionary Society, now known as OMS International.

a part of the things I criticize. When I say anything critical or negative about American Christianity, I bear part of the responsibility for the charge that I am making.

I have lived in every quarter of the twentieth century. As we come to the end of this century, I find myself deeply concerned about America and about the Body of Christ in America.

On the other hand, I thank God for those of you who are not American. It may well be that the salvation of the Body of Christ in America depends on you. We have much to learn from you, so do not hold back what God has for you to say to us. America needs to hear the voice of God again, and you may be the means for Him to speak.

The Triumph and Failure of Evangelicalism

The evangelical world today has changed from what it was when I was young and lived in the Bible Belt of the American South. I remember the day I went as a teenager to my pastor and told him that I had found Christ. This alumnus of Duke and Yale stared at me and then said with some apprehension, "You don't think this ought to happen to everybody, do you?" Suddenly, I knew I was an outsider.

I visited Duke University, our church's university in my home state, which my father helped to support through his payments to the church. I was a graduate of Asbury College and Asbury Theological Seminary, so I asked the dean for the privilege of taking one graduate course in Plato.

"Well, I don't know whether we ought to let a fellow like you take that course in Plato," he scowled. "I know what you'll do. You'll work like a dog, make a halfway decent grade, and then think you're a candidate for admission to Duke University. But I don't know if we want to give Duke degrees to Asbury men."

You see, when I attended Asbury Theological Seminary in 1944, there was not a single Ph.D. on the faculty and we had only 70 students. All of us lived in one building, which we now call Larabee-Morris. Today, Asbury is one of the largest seminaries in North America and virtually all of its faculty members have doctoral degrees. What has happened to Asbury Theological Seminary is a parable of what has happened to the entire evangelical church in the United States. We have grown up.

In 1944, the greatest seminary in the United States was Union Theological Seminary in New York City. The center of ecclesiastical power was the National Council of Churches at 475 Riverside Drive in New York. There was nothing like the National Association of Evangelicals; there was no national evangelical group in America. Evangelicals were a despised marginal group.

That has changed dramatically. The focus of power has shifted.

In those days, if the President of the United States was interested in getting spiritual counsel, he turned to the kind of church leadership represented by the National Council of Churches. But today, Billy Graham sleeps in the White House. The President attends a prayer breakfast every year that is sponsored by an evangelical group.

There were no evangelical radio broadcasts in 1944; there were no evangelical TV programs. There was hardly a Christian bookstore to be found. Now you can seldom drive outside the reach of a Christian radio station in the United States, and in any sizeable city you will find several Christian bookstores.

I believe it was 1988 when I noticed an article on the front page of the *Wall Street Journal* concerning the growth of Christian bookstores in the United States. If I remember correctly, the article said that sales of Christian books in the United States would total about 1.7 billion dollars in 1988 and would climb to 9 billion dollars by 1998. So it was not surprising to learn that, about that same time, the media entrepreneur Rupert Murdoch bought Zondervan Publishing House. By so doing, he bought his way into Christian bookstores. I doubt that Mr. Murdoch did this because of any desire to spread the Gospel. He did it to capitalize on the movement toward evangelicalism in America.

So we evangelicals have reached center stage in America in a way that some of us could not have dreamed. We give God thanks for that. What opportunities we have!

But while we have taken center stage, the moral life of our country has collapsed. Look at our political leadership in America. Many of our leaders are hardly models for anyone in the world, in terms of their personal ethics.

The same thing is true of the church. Rather than being models of virtue, too many ministers make headlines because of their reprehensible personal behavior.

As the evangelical movement has gotten stronger, the moral influence of the church as a whole has gotten weaker. I believe that part of the reason for this state of affairs is the way in which we have presented the gospel in the United States. We have engaged in a kind of reductionism concerning what we say that Jesus Christ came to do for us when He died on the cross.

I am convinced that Christ died to do a lot more for us, individually and corporately, than many of us have preached. This came into focus for me rather sharply as I prepared for this conference and began thinking about my association with foreign missionaries across the years.

Another Vision of Christianity

When I found Christ, I did not know another person in my high school or in my church who professed an experience of the new birth, except my parents. But my experience of the living Christ was so transforming that I knew the whole world needed Him. This conviction drew me to the message of Christian missions, so I found myself becoming active in a Student Volunteer prayer meeting at Asbury College.

You may be aware that the Student Volunteer Movement was responsible for sending more Christian missionaries overseas than any other movement in Christian history. The last Student Volunteer prayer meetings were held on Asbury's campus, and it existed a long time after the Student Volunteer Movement itself had officially ceased to exist. Five days a week, from 12:30 to 1:00, we students met to pray for the world.

In those meetings, I learned that many missionaries in the Far East were being held in Chinese prisoner-of-war camps. The two fellows who sat beside me in chapel services were Elmer and Ernie Kilbourne, since we were seated alphabetically. Their missionary parents were in prisoner-of-war camps in China. I often wondered what was happening to them. Then the *U.S.S. Gripsholme* brought the Kilbournes home. I had a chance to meet Dr. and Mrs. Ed Kilbourne, Elmer and Ernie's parents, because they came immediately to see their sons. When I met Hazel Kilbourne, she talked personally to me about what I would do with my life. I never quite forgot that.

Then I met Bill Gillam, a missionary to Latin America. He was an amazing person. He had lived there at a time when Catholics persecuted the Protestants, sometimes stoning them. Bill lived through a bit of that terror.

These people were heroes in my book. I listened intently when they spoke. I noticed something different about them. There was a contagious joy within them and an abandonment of self which I didn't find in most people who were around me. They talked as if they didn't mind being prisoners in China, as long as they were imprisoned for the right purpose and God was with them. They did not come home as beaten, discouraged people. They came home as radiant, witnessing people who seemed to say, "Wouldn't you like to live like this?" That was a rather strange idea to me, but I got it.

I noticed that these missionaries used a different terminology than I did. I knew about commitment, but they talked about a "total commitment." I knew something about personal surrender, but they talked about "complete surrender." We Christian students often talked about consecration. The missionaries talked about a "full consecration." We talked about sanctification; they talked about "entire sanctification." I can remember the terror those adjectives brought to me—you know, those words *full, total, entire,* and *complete.* I was a believer; I knew Christ. But I kept a finger on a corner of my life and I wanted to do a little bargaining with God about what He did with me. As those missionaries talked about their lives, something inside of me said there had to be a complete abandonment of myself, similar to what I saw in them and to which they bore witness, if I was to know God's grace as they knew it.

I thank God for that, because I doubt that I would be standing here today if it wasn't for their message of God's total demand upon my life. When a person loses control of himself and rests totally in the hands of God, he then finds himself. So, as I anticipated this week of conferences, I found myself thinking back to those foreign missionaries and their influence upon me. I found myself giving thanks to God for those who shared something with me that I did not find elsewhere in America.

I am convinced that, in America, *we have largely preached the gospel of Christ as a way to find freedom from the consequences of our sin, rather than freedom from the sin that causes those consequences.* We have preached a narrow kind of gospel that has been largely confined to the questions, "How can I get rid of this load of guilt that I bear? What will happen to me when I die?"

Of course, no one wants to live with guilt. Everyone wants to be free from a guilty conscience. So we have preached the message that Christ can forgive sins. We have held out the hope that a person can be in a position where he does not fear death. We have given the impression that this is the essence of the Christian message. Our society has gotten that idea from us.

A commentator who was recently interviewing Billy Graham on national TV said, "I envy you."

"Why would you envy me?" Billy asked.

"Because of your peace," the commentator said. "I'm terrified at the thought of dying, and you seem so confident about it all."

Freedom from the fear of death is important. And who would not like to escape hell? So we have preached salvation as a means of escape, a way to avoid the consequences of sin, a plan to bypass eternal judgment. We have preached a "gospel" with a selfish appeal, and I think we are paying a high price for that kind of reductionism.

When I looked at Hazel Kilbourne just after she returned from China, I noticed that her legs were bowed because she had lived for years on a handful of rice a day. The rice had lost most of its nutrients as it was cooked. Yet she did not complain about that.

When it was time for Bill Gillam to return to Latin America, he knew he was going to face persecution, possibly stoning. He debated whether he should stay home in the safety of the United States. As he prayed that summer, God set him free from self-concern. He went back to face the persecutors, went back to face them victoriously and joyously. I saw the change that took place in him.

When another missionary named Annie Cartozian stayed in our home, we found that she was a brilliant, well-educated woman. She had boundless energy, drive, and mental alertness. She also had a taste for the finer things of life. She was a refined, cultured person. She told us how she had escaped from her enemies three times, taking only what she could carry in her hands, nothing more.

I asked, "How do you feel when you lose everything you have?"

She looked at me with a wry sort of grin and said, "Well, you find out what's important! You learn that your enemies can never take away from you anything that really counts."

In such people, I saw a Christianity that could change the world.

As I talked with these people, a question began to run in my mind: *Does Christ want to do something more than just save my skin?*

John 17 says that Jesus, facing the cross on the last night of his earthly life, said, "Now this is eternal life: that they might know you, the only true God, and Jesus Christ, whom you have sent" (John 17:3). In other words, God wants me simply to know Him. That is what Christianity has to offer the world, a personal relationship with God, not an escape route from judgment.

The Courtroom Metaphor of Salvation

It's difficult for us to realize this in America, because we have allowed one biblical metaphor to control our thinking about salvation. That metaphor is a courtroom scene, given to us in Scripture to illustrate justification by faith. (See Heb. 10:26–36).

I remember a notable example of that metaphor in a sermon by Henry Clay Morrison, who founded Asbury Theological Seminary. Morrison told how he had broken the law when he was a youth. He ended up in court, sitting next to a burly, blue-uniformed police officer who held him in custody. The judge on the bench called Morrison's case. The judge then turned to the prosecuting attorney and asked, "Does he have a defender?"

The prosecuting attorney said, "No, your honor. He doesn't have a lawyer to defend him."

The judge said, "He must have a defense." He looked down at a group of young lawyers in the court room, pointed to one and called him by name, then said, "You be his defender."

"So I sat there in the dock, next to the uniformed policeman," Morrison said. "That young attorney walked over and sat down next to me. He asked me, 'Are you guilty? Did you really do what they say you did?'

"'Oh,' I told him, 'I did a lot more than they arrested me for!'

"The young lawyer said, 'Well, then, the best thing you can do is throw yourself on the mercy of the court.'"

Morrison said, "There was something so winsome about that young lawyer that when he said, 'You had better throw yourself on the mercy of the court,' I felt confident in him. I thought that, if he was going to do the 'throwing,' I was willing for him to throw me anywhere. He was my only hope.

"So the attorney said to the judge, 'Your honor, my client pleads guilty.'

"Then something extraordinary happened. The attorney continued by saying, 'Father, if you will just turn this young man over to me and let me take care of him, I will see that he never appears in your court again.'"

Henry Clay Morrison said, "I heard that word, *Father*, and thought, *Can it be?* I looked at the judge and knew it was true. My defense lawyer was the judge's son, so I knew everything was going to be all right."

That was a magnificent sermon and many people found Christ through it. But notice the context of Morrison's illustration. It is a legal scene: a judge on the bench, a book of law, a violation of the law, a uniformed policeman, and the son of the judge, like the Son of God who pleads our case and takes our penalty. When Morrison got to the end of that sermon, he explained these figures of speech. He said, "You know, this didn't happen in the county court; it was in a little Methodist church. The uniformed officer was the Holy Ghost, who held me under conviction. And the young lawyer was the eternal Son of God."

This legal metaphor, valid though it is, remains but one of several that the Bible uses to express the relationship that God wants us to have with Him, a relationship that the Cross of Christ made possible. We don't have time to develop all of these metaphors here, but let us look at a few of them.

The Metaphor of Friendship

The first biblical metaphor for our relationship with God is not justification by faith. In order to have that, we must have a law book and a legal system. Long before there was any legal system, the Bible uses a different metaphor to describe the relationship between a human being and God. That metaphor appears in the book of Genesis, as it describes God's relationship with Abraham. Though Paul identifies Abraham as the best example of justification by faith (Rom. 4:1-2), Abraham never knew the Law (Rom 4:13). He never heard of the Ten Commandments. In fact, Abraham never knew the sacrificial system of the Old Testament. He never read a Bible and knew nothing about the church. So how does Genesis describe how Abraham lived in relationship with God?

It seems to me that the key word in Genesis is not *obey* or *believe*, but it is *walk*. You will remember how, at the cool of the day, God walked with Adam and Eve (Gen. 3:8). You will remember how Enoch walked with God and he was no more, because God just took him home (Gen. 5:24). You will remember that God saw the world when it was full of evil, and He thought, *I've got to make a new start. Where can I find someone with whom I can start?* Genesis says He found "a righteous man, blameless among the people of his time, and he walked with God" (Gen. 6:9)—a man named Noah.

I had read that text about Noah for years and now I believe I misread it. I assumed that Noah was upright and blameless, *therefore* he walked with God. But now I am convinced that Noah was upright and blameless *because* he walked with God. He was upright and blameless *as a result of* walking with God. Until a person knows fellowship with the living Lord, he cannot be delivered from the self-interest that tyrannizes him, contaminating his life and relationships.

But Noah walked with God. As he did, a measure of the very character of God was transferred to him. There was a nobility about Noah that caused God to say, "I can make a new start with this man."

Likewise, when God made His covenant with Abraham, He said, "Walk before Me and be thou perfect" (Gen. 17:1, KJV). So the biblical picture of Abraham's relationship with God was one of walking with Him. It is a metaphor of friendship. If you look at 2 Chronicles 20:7, Isaiah 41:8, and James 2:23, you will find that Abraham is called the "friend" of God. So the first metaphor that Scripture gives for our relationship with God is something as simple as friendship.

The only people with whom I take walks are people I like or people I want to know intimately. That's the picture we get of Abraham's relationship with God. Abraham liked God. (I'm using the word *like* instead of *love* because we've trafficked in the latter word so much that it often is meaningless.) God liked Abraham and said, "Walk with Me." So we see in Genesis a God who likes human beings and wants the kind of relationship with them that induces Him to walk with them.

When we get to the Book of Exodus, we see how God's people received the Law (Ex. 34:1-32). Here we encounter the background for the Bible's teaching of justification by faith.

The Metaphor of Family

However, as we move through the rest of the Pentateuch, we find that a third metaphor begins to develop. It's the metaphor of a family. I believe that the first time God is called "Father" in the Bible is Exodus 4. That is where God tells Moses, "Then say to Pharaoh, 'This is what the Lord says: Israel is my firstborn son, and I told you, "Let my son go, so he may worship me." But you refused to let him go; so I will kill your firstborn son'" (Ex. 4:22-23). God calls the people of Israel His child, His son. Here is the beginning of the family concept that is so fully developed in the New Testament, where Christ instructs His followers to begin their prayers by saying, "Our Father" (Matt. 6:9; Luke 11:2).

For centuries, theologians have placed a primary emphasis on the sovereignty of God. Yet the Apostles' Creed begins with, "I believe in God the Father Almighty." God is called the *Father* before the term *Almighty* is applied to Him. This family relationship is in the very nature of deity, because God is the Father of Christ the Son, and He desires to have with every human being a relationship like the one He has with His eternal Son.

Scripture repeatedly emphasizes this expression of "God the Father," saying that He wants a relationship with us like He has with Jesus Christ, His Son. So we get adopted into His family (cf. Gal. 4:5; Eph. 1:4-5). We are "born again" (John 3:3; 1 Pet. 1:23). His Spirit within our hearts cries out, "Abba, Father" (Gal. 4:6). What an intimate relationship this is!

I remember the story of a woman whose husband had been a member of the cabinet of Pakistan. She met two Baptist missionaries who gave her a New Testament. She began to get spiritually hungry, but the thing that held her back from becoming a Christian was the Lord's Prayer, because she could not bring herself to call Allah her "Father." She knew that if she called Allah "Father," she would be using a human designation for the supreme God, who would destroy her for being blasphemous. But her heart got so hungry that she ultimately said, "Father." Although she was a dignified woman, she immediately fell prostrate on the floor, expecting to be struck dead. Instead she heard a gentle voice saying to her heart, *Daughter... Daughter... Daughter....*

As we move on in the Old Testament, we begin to see another metaphor used to describe our relationship with God. God says to the prophet Hosea, "Go, take to yourself an adulterous wife... because the land is guilty of the vilest adultery in departing from the Lord" (Hos. 1:2). Here we see the beginning of the concept of the people of God as the spouse of God.

The Metaphor of Marriage

Ezekiel 16 sets forth a summary of Israel's history, in which God says:

> Your ancestry and birth were in the land of the Canaanites; your father was an Amorite and your mother a Hittite. On the day you were born your cord was not cut, nor were you washed with water to make you clean.... Rather, you were thrown out into the open field, for on the day you were born you were despised.
>
> Then I passed by and saw you kicking about in your blood, and as you lay there in your blood I said to you, "Live!" I made you grow.... You grew up and developed and became the most beautiful of jewels....
>
> Later I passed by, and when I looked at you and saw that you were old enough for love, I spread the corner of my garment over you and covered your nakedness. I gave you my solemn oath and entered into a covenant with you, declares the Sovereign Lord, and you became mine (Eze. 16:3b-8).

The New Testament continues this marital metaphor of our relationship with God. Our story began with the wedding of Adam and Eve, and it ends with the marriage supper of the Lamb. The Apostle John writes:

> I saw the Holy City, the new Jerusalem, coming down out of heaven from God, prepared as a bride dressed for her husband. And I heard a loud voice from the throne saying, "Now the dwelling of God is with men, and he will live with them. They will be his people, and God himself will be with them and be their God. He will wipe every tear from their eyes. There will be no more death or mourning or crying or pain, for the old order of things has passed away" (Rev. 21:2-4).

So the most intimate relationship that we have—the relationship of wife and husband—is used as a symbol of that greater, deeper, and more intimate relationship we are to have with God.

I believe that human marriage, human parenthood, and childhood are all metaphors of that other, eternal relationship. God is our eternal Father. There will be no marriages in heaven because all of us will be "like angels," married to the Lamb of God (cf. Matt. 22:30-32, NKJV).

I remember standing in front of an altar in a Methodist church in Schenectady, New York, and saying, "I do." As Elsie and I walked out of that church, Elsie left her father and her mother and her home (she was a Yankee) to become a Southerner. If you are not an American, you may not understand the significance of that; but let me tell you, it was a radical cultural shift for her! Elsie left all of her financial security and other things to become the wife of a preacher. (My salary at the time was $750 a year.) She left it all to be with me.

In effect, God says, "That's what I want you to do with Me."

Interestingly, the marriage metaphor isn't the ultimate metaphor of our life with God. When we reach the Gospels, we find an even deeper intimacy described. We see this in Paul's writings (e.g., Col. 2:9-12), but we find it most specifically delineated in Revelation 3:20, where Christ says, "Here I am! I stand at the door and knock. If anyone hears my voice and opens the door, I will come in and eat with him, and he with me." So not only can we say, "Christ is with us," but He wants to be in us.

The Metaphor of Indwelling

Elsie can drive me to an airport and watch me fly off to Timbuktu, leaving her behind. But God says, "I want a relationship closer than that. What I really would like is this: Wherever you go, I go. If I go, you will go there, too."

This kind of intimacy is even closer than that of a husband and wife. This is called "living in Christ."

I ran across a book recently that said the most important theological expression in Scripture is the prefix, *in-*. The author wrote a sentence that had eight or ten theological words containing the prefix, *in-*, words like *incarnation, indwelling,* and *inhabit*. The wonder of the gospel is "Christ *in* you, the hope of glory" (Col. 1:27, italics added).

However, even this is not the deepest expression of the relationship God wants with us. If you read the Gospels and the epistles of Paul carefully, you'll find there is a closer one.

The Metaphor of Identity

I skipped over this for years because it was too difficult for me to comprehend. The metaphor first occurs in Matthew 10:17-42, where Jesus sends out the Twelve to preach. He says, in essence, "Fellows, it's not going to be easy. They're going to haul you into court. They'll persecute you and mistreat you."

Finally, He says, "He who receives you receives me, and he who receives me receives the one who sent me" (Matt. 10:40).

What He is describing is not mere *inhabitation*. It's getting close to *identity*, isn't it? Christ and the believer are so closely identified that when you receive a believer, you receive Christ. If you reject a believer, you reject Christ. If you get Christ, you get the Father; and if you miss Him, you miss the Father.

I used to read this passage and say, *Thank God, I wasn't one of the apostles!*

Then I read Luke 10, where Jesus sends out seventy-two disciples. He says essentially the same thing to them: "He who listens to you listens to me; he who rejects you rejects me; but he who rejects me rejects him who sent me" (Luke 10:16).

I thought, *Thank God, I wasn't one of them!*

Then I read the account of the Last Supper in John 13, where Jesus says this will be true of every believer: "I tell you the truth, whoever accepts anyone I send accepts me; and whoever accepts me accepts the one who sent me" (John 13:20).

You know, I think this is what Paul meant when he said, "For to me, to live is Christ" (Phil. 1:21). I've always been impressed by that verse and wanted to use it as my life verse, but I was afraid it might seem a bit arrogant. For me to live, that is Christ? Sure, Christ is life for me. But this also means I am to be Christ to other people. I was not sure I wanted this. I thought it would be arrogant for me to say that I did.

Paul says this without a blink. He can do so because he says something else:

> But thanks be to God, who always leads us in triumphal procession in Christ and through us spreads everywhere the fragrance of the knowledge of him. For we are to God the aroma of Christ among those who are being saved and those who are perishing. To the one we are the smell of death; to the other, the fragrance of life.

And who is equal to such a task? Unlike so many, we do not peddle the word of God for profit. On the contrary, in Christ we speak before God with sincerity, like men sent from God (2 Cor. 2:14–16).

That opening statement, "Thanks be to God who always leads us in triumphal procession," is very interesting to me. Most commentators relate this statement to the resurrection. They say Christ came out of the empty tomb to lead us in triumphal procession to heaven. But then Paul says, "Through us [He] spreads everywhere the fragrance of the knowledge of him."

John Calvin said Paul must have confused his metaphors at this point, because you can't extract fragrance from anything until it is crushed, totally crushed. Calvin reasoned that the crushing must be a metaphor of the Cross, but that would mean Paul put the Resurrection ahead of the Cross. Surely, Calvin thought, the Apostle was confused.

But if you trace the meaning of the Greek word used here for "triumphal procession," you find it describes a military parade in which the person leading the procession is finally sacrificed to the god of the victor. So Paul did not confuse his metaphors. There is only one metaphor, and it is the Cross all the way through. When you and I come to the place where we die to ourselves and wholly belong to Christ, then it is possible for a fragrance to effuse from us, which will draw people to Christ.

Let me say this in closing: I believe that in America we preach the gospel in such a way that the concept of entire sanctification or perfection of love appears to be tacked onto salvation—a sort of optional blessing. But how can we become the means of spreading the aroma of Christ in this world, if there is any uncrucified self left within us? Only when we come to the end of ourselves can He become manifest.

I believe we need to think more clearly about what Christ intended when He died for us on the Cross. What an amazing thought, that God could bring us into intimacy with himself—the very kind of intimacy that exists between the Father, Son, and Holy Spirit! How is such a thing possible? Only through the cleansing blood of Jesus Christ and the sanctifying power of His Holy Spirit within us.

Then, wherever we are, Christ is there.

Our Father, we pray that You will stretch our hearts and our minds until we see the fullness of Your will for us. Help us to see that Your will for us is greater—often far greater—than many of us have imagined. Let not any part of the sacrifice of the Cross have been given in vain, but let us know the full benefits of the atonement of Christ, so that we will give You praise in Christ's name. Amen.

Anyone inquiring of the Lord would go to the tent of meeting outside the camp. And whenever Moses went out to the tent, all the people rose and stood at the entrances to their tents, watching Moses until he entered the tent. As Moses went into the tent, the pillar of cloud would come down and stay at the entrance, while the Lord spoke with Moses....

Moses said to the Lord, "You have been telling me, 'Lead these people,' but you have not let me know whom you will send with me. You have said, 'I know you by name and you have found favor with me.' If you are pleased with me, teach me your ways so I may know you and continue to find favor with you. Remember that this nation is your people."

The Lord replied, "My Presence will go with you, and I will give you rest."

Then Moses said to him, "If your Presence does not go with us, do not send us up from here. How will anyone know that you are pleased with me and with your people unless you go with us? What else will distinguish me and your people from all the other people on the face of the earth?"

—Exodus 33:7-9, 12-16

2. Confronting Our Sin

CHRISTIANITY is an historical faith. We believe God started history. We are not among those who believe that the universe is eternal; instead, we believe God created it. We do not believe that time is cyclical; rather, we believe that historical progress is possible because God started time and He will end it.

We Christians believe that human history essentially is good, because God himself decided to step into it. In the second Person of the blessed Trinity, He took upon himself earthly physical form. The sanctity of all of physical creation comes from the One who made it and sustains it.

But for Christians, there is a troublesome problem with history, too—isn't there? We say that the God who made the cosmos and the historical process is good. In fact, we say that He is goodness itself. We say that He is in sovereign control of our world. But if God reigns over the cosmos, if He will bring it to culmination in His own time and in His own way, how can it be that the world is in such a mess?

At the start of the twenty-first century, we Americans are pondering how different the moral and spiritual atmosphere of the United States is now, compared to what it was one hundred years ago. The difference is reflected in the ironic title of a magazine that once was the paramount ecumenical Christian voice in the United States. The magazine was founded in 1897. With the year 1900 approaching, the founders decided to call it *The Christian Century* because they believed that the twentieth century would be thoroughly Christian. They were confident we would have no more war. We would have no more international hostility. We would have no more of any of the things that eventually did characterize the twentieth century. Those religious leaders hoped that the twentieth century would especially reflect the spirit of Jesus Christ.

Then came the First World War. It was followed by Adolph Hitler, Auschwitz, Belsen, and the horrors of World War II. Then came the Korean War and the war in Vietnam. The twentieth century revealed that all of the problems of mankind are still with us.

What went wrong? If a good God is in control of this world, how do we explain what has happened?

The Problem of Evil

The existence of evil in the world is a more intense problem for Christians than for other people, because we believe the world did not begin this way. The Scriptures tell us that human life began in a Garden. We know that a garden is a place of order and beauty. It is normally a place of tranquility and fruitfulness. It is a place of refreshment. That is how our world begin, according to the Bible, but that is not the way it is today. (Many of you who live in Third World countries know this better than we Americans.)

The problem gets worse because we Christians also believe that the world will not end this way. We expect to live in a City that will not be like our present human cities. It will be a Holy City that comes down out of heaven from God. In this City, there will be no suffering, no sorrow, no pain, no death, no tears (Rev. 21:4). There will be joy like that at a wedding feast (Rev. 19:7-9). We believe this will be the culmination of human history.

If we believe our world started well and it is going to end well, how did it get the way it is? And how can it be righted?

Many people would explain our predicament in terms of demonic forces, and we certainly do believe in a demonic realm. Some thinkers have explained it by supposing that physical matter is evil in itself, so that we have an ongoing conflict between the good spirit and the evil flesh. But we Christians, if we are true to Scripture, must explain the evil of our world on a very different ground, one that unbelievers have great difficulty in understanding.

The Book of Genesis tells us that the Fall, the cause of all evil, resulted from an incredibly simple thing. It was as simple as turning one's face. Given the seriousness of our current problem, we are inclined to think there must have been a great evil of such enormity that it cast its destructive shadow across every page of human history since. No! The book of Genesis says that our forebears simply turned their attention away from the One who came to walk with them and talk with them in the cool of the day. They became preoccupied with a gift that He had given them. They became more enamored of the gift than with the God who gave it.

In essence, God had said, "Everything here is yours. But I want you to know only good, so you must focus your attention on Me, the Source of all goodness. If you turn your attention away from Me, you will see what evil is. And if you let your source of life become anything other than Me, you will come to know the difference between good and evil" (cf. Gen. 2:15-17).

In biblical terms, *evil* is not something that is wrong in itself. It is simply good that we place out of proper relationship to the Creator who made it—something which God made to enrich our lives, not to destroy or deplete our lives. This is a revolutionary concept among the religions of the world. This understanding of the origin of evil has been at the heart of Christianity's challenge to every other religious system.

What are we saying? That God is good and He is a Person. We are saying that goodness is summed up in a Person whose name we know. He has given His name to us and He has invited us to live in unbroken communion with Him.

It is very easy for us to think of sin as a violation of the Law, but remember that Abraham lived

The Nature of Sin

his whole life without ever knowing about the Law. The Law came with Moses. Before the giving of the Law, God said to human beings, "I have only one condition for our relationship. Keep that condition and let Me be who I am supposed to be, the Center and Source of your life." But we turned away.

Isaiah 53:6 gives us a matchless definition of sin as it speaks about the sacrifice of Christ. For a long time, I missed the simplicity of it. Sometimes it is so easy to see the complicated, yet miss the simple and obvious. The Scripture says, "All we like sheep have gone astray; we have all turned to our own way, and the Lord has laid on him the iniquity of us all" (NRSV).

The sin of the world is simply the consequence of "turning to our own way," rejecting the One whose face we are supposed to seek and in whose light we are supposed to live. Martin Luther expressed it in a very graphic way. He defined sin as *cor incurvatus ad se:*

> *cor* = the heart
> *incurvatus* = turned in
> *ad se* = upon itself

So Luther, understanding the biblical concept, said that the essence of sin is my turning away from the One from whom I came, turning instead to myself in an effort to find what I need. It's the effort to "do it my way." When I do that, all sorts of evil becomes possible because I have turned away from the Source of all that is good. I have turned away from the Lord.

As I said, this concept is not easy to accept. Sin is simply that I have begun to live for myself; I have turned within. I try to find out who I am by turning to myself rather than to God. I will find out who you are by turning to myself rather than turning to Him. I will find out what will satisfy me by turning within instead of turning to Him.

By contrast, there is an eccentricity about the person who is a true believer. The believer's life is centered outside of himself, in the One from whom he came and to whom he goes, in the One with whom he walks each day.

Can this really be the explanation of how evil entered our world? Could evil result from our own choice to follow ourselves rather than God?

If we think about life biblically, we must say yes, this explains it all. Scripture teaches that God is the source of all light. "In the beginning God created the heavens and the earth. Now the earth was formless and empty, darkness was over the surface of the deep, and the Spirit of God was hovering over the waters. And God said, 'Let there be light,' and there was light" (Gen. 1:1-3).

Turning Away from the Light

This is directly analogous to the promise we have received in Jesus Christ. Into the darkness of the world, God sent His Son, His Word. His Son said, "I am the light of the world" (John 8:12). In other words, "When I come to you, you will understand who you are. You will know who your brother is, when I come to you. You will know who your enemy is, when I come to you. You will know what life really is, when I come to you. You will understand and see clearly. If you cut yourself off from Me, the shadows will begin to fall."

Each of us knows by experience what it is to turn our backs on the light we had received, to find ourselves with shadows falling across life's pathway. The farther we got from the light, the deeper the darkness became. It is therefore significant that Jesus' expression for hell is "outer darkness" (Matt. 8:12; 22:13; 25:30, NKJV).

In America, we often preach that Hell is a place of judgment where God is going to "get even" with us for taking our lives into our own hands and pushing Him to the margin. There is none of this vindictive teaching in Scripture, so far as I can find. Christ simply states a fact when He says that He is the Source of all light—intellectual, moral, spiritual light. So when we turn away from Him, the

Turning Away from the Truth

shadows begin to fall. On the other hand, if we know that He is the Source of our light, then there is no reason for us to walk into the "outer darkness." There is no reason to live in delusion or illusion. Only when the connection between us and our Source is broken, only then does the darkness move in.

Human history is admittedly a dark story. But Christ brings light, because He brings truth. He is not only the divine Son, but the "Sun" who illuminates how we should live. When Jesus came, He not only came to *give* us truth. He said, "I am...the truth" (John 14:6). All too often, truth seems abstract for us; but Jesus demonstrated that truth is a Person. It is summed up in Him. And when He comes into your life, truth comes in (cf. John 18:37-38).

The Scriptures illustrate this point in many passages. One of these is Isaiah 59, in which God describes what He sees in Jerusalem, the Holy City. God finds that darkness has encompassed His own people, who were to be a light to the world. Isaiah says,

> So justice is far from us,
>   and righteousness does not reach us.
> We look for light, but all is darkness;
>   for brightness, but we walk in deep shadows.
> Like the blind we grope along the wall,
>   feeling our way like men without eyes.
> At midday we stumble as if it were twilight;
>   among the strong, we are like the dead.
> We all growl like bears;
>   we moan mournfully like doves.
> We look for justice, but find none;
>   for deliverance, but it is far away
>   (Isa. 59:9-11).

Why? Because we have separated ourselves from our Source of truth. This reminds me of a line from the modern philosopher Nietzsche, who said that someone who seeks God is like a madman who carries a lighted lantern in broad daylight.[1] But when we lose the Light, we must look for any help we can find. Only when God's Holy Spirit comes can we see the truth (John 16:13).

What is truth? I recently pulled down a dictionary to trace the etymology of the English word, *true*. It comes from an old Indo-European word, *treow*, which meant "tree."

Why would a tree be a symbol for truth? I think of two oak trees in our front yard. They hold their leaves for six months, dropping them one at a time, so that I have to rake leaves every week for half the year! But when I am not raking leaves, I think they are lovely. I asked myself, *How are those trees like truth?* It suddenly dawned on me. Never have I gone to bed wondering where one of those trees would be the next morning. In all the years we've lived at that house, neither of those trees has moved. They don't budge. That's the way truth is.

That's the way God is. You can count on Him. He doesn't change. Faithfulness and truth come together in Almighty God.

In Hebrew, the word for "believe" and the word for "faith" come from the same linguistic root, which is also the source of the Hebrew word for "truth." That Hebrew root word is *amen*, which we use at the end of our prayers to mean, "Let it be so. Let it be true. Let it be unchangeable. Let it be established." The Hebrew word for "truth" is *emmenet*, though it always appears in the contracted form, *ement*. It comes from that root word, *amen*.

In other words, the ancient Hebrews knew that truth does not change. It is something we can count on.

A university student once asked me, "Dr. Kinlaw, if you take any academic discipline—whether it is history, chemistry, biology, English literature, the

---

[1]Friedrich Nietzsche, *The Gay Science*, Walter Kaufmann, ed. (New York: Vintage, 1974), pp.181-82.

French language, or whatever—and you push it far enough, you'll come to the study of philosophy, won't you?"

I said, "Yes, that's right. In the Western world, one academic degree is paramount in every discipline: the Doctor of Philosophy degree. Whether you are going to teach French, biology, history or geography, the highest degree in your chosen field will be a Doctor of Philosophy degree."

"And if you push philosophy far enough, you'll be in theology, won't you?" he asked.

"Yes, that's right."

"And if you push theology far enough, you will come to the center of all knowledge, won't you?"

I said, "Yes."

This university senior smiled and said, "Now *that's* what I'd like to study!"

And I said, *Thank You, Lord.*

If you have the Center of life, everything else will fall into place. But when you lose the Center, everything else begins to come apart. When we lose communion with God, it is little wonder that our world disintegrates and our personal lives unravel. Our marriages disintegrate, our friendships disintegrate, our organizations disintegrate, even our best-planned programs disintegrate.

Moses understood this. Facing the prospect of leading the Israelites out of Egypt, he said to God, "If your Presence does not go with us, do not send us up from here" (Ex. 33:15).

Turning Away from the Sacred

Not only is God the Source of light and truth, but He is the Source of everything sacred. When God made you and me, He placed within us a sense of the sacredness of life. Even a person who holds nothing else to be sacred still wants to be treated as someone special. Something within each of us cries out that we are persons of value and significance. That sense comes from God. But if we turn away from Him, life becomes profane. Everything has the same value, because our values are gone.

We can treat a person like an animal or treat an animal like a person.

Do you know the story of the eighteenth-century Englishman William Wilberforce? He came from a wealthy family and had enough money to fritter away most of his days at the university. But after graduation, he ran for Parliament and was elected.

Soon afterward, his mother persuaded him to accompany his sister and her on a trip to the Rivera. They traveled by horse-drawn coach. Can you imagine how long it took for a team of horses to pull a coach from the English Channel to the Mediterranean? Wilberforce dreaded the thought of being cooped up with his mother and sister that long, so he arranged for them to take two coaches instead of one. He then invited a friend to ride in the second coach with him.

"We ought to have something good to read," he told his friend. So they borrowed a copy of Philip Doddridge's *The Rise and Progress of Religion in the Soul*, an autobiographical novel on the work of God's grace in a person's heart. By the time they finished reading that book on their trip to the Mediterranean, William Wilberforce decided there must truly be a God.

The next year, he had to take another trip with his mother, so he invited a man named Isaac Middler to accompany them. Wilberforce asked him what they should read on the journey. Isaac Middler was a devout Christian, so he said, "Let's take the New Testament—the Greek New Testament." That was quite a challenge!

By the time they returned to London, William Wilberforce was a fervent believer in Jesus Christ. Christ had become the Center of his life.

Do you know what happened then? Wilberforce told the members of Parliament that the color of a person's skin doesn't matter; every person is made in the image of God. He said that a person's place of origin doesn't matter, whether from England or from Africa, because every person is made in the image of God. Wilberforce told Parliament that Britain's slaves had to be freed. He fought for the abolition of slavery for fifty years. Just a few weeks before his death, the slaves of Britain were indeed set free.

Why did that happen? Because one man met Jesus Christ. Certainly, other factors figured into the end of the slave trade, but this one man fought the battle unrelentingly. He came habitually from his quiet time of prayer into the sessions of Parliament. His faith in Christ determined his political stand. Light came into his life, and people who formerly had been treated like things became sacred to him.

I believe our world today needs nothing less than this. Our sense of the sacredness of human life comes from God, because He alone is holy. He alone gives worth to our lives. If we lose our relationship with Him, nothing has any value to us. But when we recognize that our personhood comes from Him, then we must treat our personhood as a divine gift with eternal significance.

Turning Away from Love

When you turn away from God, you turn away from more than God. You turn away from Light, turn away from Truth, and turn away from the Sacred. You also turn away from Love. This subject is difficult to discuss, because we use the word *love* to describe so many different realities. In fact, we may use that word to express contradictory things.

I can recall the days of my courtship. I first became conscious of Elsie in a Monday night prayer meeting. On Tuesday morning after chapel service, I leaned against the radiator at the campus post office and waited for her to come and get her mail. I can still see her as she came. She walked past and paid no attention to me. She walked to the mailbox, bent over, opened the box, removed her mail, then walked down the corridor and around the corner. I can still tell you what she was wearing.

My life was suddenly reoriented. I learned which dormitory room she lived in. It was on the east side of the girls' dormitory, so I began walking down to the cemetery on a regular basis in order to walk back and look up at Elsie's room. Then I began finding excuses to bump into her. There was an eccentric element in my life now. I was off-center because Elsie had become important to me.

One day, I said to her, "I love you. Will you marry me?"

Elsie thought I was saying, "I care deeply about you." But you know what I was really saying: "I care a great deal about *myself*. When you're with me, I'm happy. The closer you are to me, the happier I am, and I like to be happy. If I could have you near me all the time, I could be very happy." Do you see what I mean about our contradictory uses of the word *love*?

Our human languages do not have a word that adequately describes the kind of love God has for us. So the New Testament writers took a word out of the everyday Greek vocabulary and transformed it. The New Testament says that, instead of having a heart curved in upon itself and its own desires, the person who experiences God's love will be turned inside out. It's a love that makes you care more about others than you care about yourself. There is only one Source of love like that, and it is not within you. It is not within me.

Even when we do good works, charitable works, we do them with a motive of self-interest. We do these things because we want to look good and feel good. That is a destructive human sentiment. A very different motive characterizes the love of God.

We see it demonstrated in the love that the divine Father has for the Son, the love that the Son has for the Father, the love that the Father and Son have for the Spirit, and the love that the Spirit has for the Father and Son. This love is other-oriented. It's the kind of love which moved the Son to lay down His life for the Father and for us.

Do you know what the world desperately needs today? It needs a love that can turn a person inside out, so that the heart is not "curved in upon itself," but cares about others more than about itself. Only the Holy Spirit can work that transformation in the human heart.

If God does not live within us, in the Person of His Holy Spirit, we will live like the rest of the world. All of our good works will have a defiling contamination. Only God is the source of genuine love. This is why we Christians say that God *is* love.

Is Love Self-Oriented or Sacrificial?

The Muslim god Allah loves the people who die for him. Other gods are said to love in other ways, but their love is always self-oriented. Because of the triune nature of the true God, wherein each Person is giving himself for the other two, we can say that God is love. He invites us to enter the intimacy of that love relationship, saying, "You can become like Us, in the sense that we care about each other more than We care about ourselves."

When Stanley Tam retired from the OMS Board of Trustees, I gave him a plaque in my capacity as chairman of the board. I felt a little foolish, giving him such a modest thing in view of his incredible generosity to the organization. When I had finished my presentation speech, he said, "May I say just a word?"

He then turned to the assembly and said, "I want to explain why I'm here. I was a door-to-door salesman when a lady led me to Christ. The love of Christ began to fill my heart. Then I met a young evangelist and he became my friend. He said, 'Stanley, you need to visit the mission field. Let me take you to Korea.'

"I found myself in Los Angeles overnight. From there, we flew to Hawaii and then to Seoul. My friend said, 'There's a lady here I'd like you to meet.' He ushered me into the apartment of Lettie B. Cowman.[2]

"I was fascinated by Mrs. Cowman. There was a regal air about her, a queenliness. I sensed that

---

[2]Lettie B. Cowman wrote the devotional classic *Streams in the Desert* and was a co-founder of OMS International.

she was a most extraordinary woman. As we came to the end of our conversation, she asked, 'Mr. Tam, may I tell you a story?'

"'Why, yes,' I said. 'Please do.'

"She said, 'When my husband and I were young, we lived in Chicago. He was a Western Union operator who managed 110 men. A man named E.A. Kilbourne sat across the desk from him....'"

Mr. Tam explained that Mrs. Cowman had been converted in a Methodist revival and then went to work on her husband. She took him to the same revival, but he didn't respond. When they got home that night, Lettie finally led him to Christ. The love of Christ began to move his soul and he soon grew more spiritually mature than Lettie was.

He continued, "They were riding on a street car one Friday afternoon when they saw a sign that said, *Missionary Conference: A.B. Simpson Speaking.* So Charlie Cowman said, 'Lettie, let's go. We've never been to a missionary conference.'

"They went that night and heard A.B. Simpson speak on the need to win a world for Christ and the sacrifice which Christ had made for the world. Charlie was deeply touched.

"At the end of the service, A.B. Simpson said, 'We must take an offering. However, this offering will be different from the rest. You will notice that the collection plates will be full of watches. They are not gold watches, but they are good watches. If you own a gold watch, I ask you to put it in the collection plate and take one of the cheaper watches out. Then we'll sell your gold watch and use the proceeds to carry the gospel to the ends of the earth.'"

Stanley Tam said, "Lettie Cowman was astounded. She had never heard of anything like this. But soon the collection plate reached them, and it was full of watches. Lettie handed it to Charlie. He took it with his left hand and held onto it. He didn't pass it along. Lettie was horrified to see him reach into his watch pocket and pull out a gold watch.

She had scrimped for months to give him that watch. He put it into the collection plate and took a cheap watch out.

"Lettie spun on him and said, 'I gave you that watch!' But by that time, the offering plate was gone.

"She said A.B. Simpson then came back to the pulpit and said, 'We must take another offering. You will notice the plates are empty this time. Many of us wear more jewelry than is necessary for good grooming. So, if you will just drop your unnecessary jewelry in the collection plate, we have arranged for a jeweler to sell it. We'll use the proceeds to send the gospel to people who have not heard it.'

"Here came the collection plate," Tam said. "Lettie Cowman handed it to Charlie. He took it with his left hand, and with his right hand he reached over to her and pulled off her diamond engagement ring, then dropped it in the collection plate.

"She spun on him again and said, 'You gave that to me!' But the collection plate was gone.

"She said A.B. Simpson came back to the pulpit and said, 'We must take another offering. This time, we will take a money offering.'

"When the collection plate came, Lettie saw Charlie reach into his coat pocket and pull out the envelope that contained two weeks' pay, which he had received that afternoon. He then dropped all of it into the collection plate—half a month's salary.

"Lettie looked at him in disbelief. 'Charlie, what are we going to live on?' she asked. But again, the plate was gone."

Stanley Tam paused in telling Mrs. Cowman's story. By this time, we were hanging on every word.

"Dr. Simpson came back to the pulpit and said, 'Now we must take the offering that really matters. We must take the offering of life. Some people here need to give their lives to Christ for service around the world. If you're willing to give your life to Christ and go to the ends of the earth with the gospel of Christ, stand up.'

"Lettie said, 'Charlie stood up. Mr. Tam, I knew Charlie well enough that, if he said he was going to go, he'd go—whether I went with him or not! I didn't want to live alone, so I stood up, too!' She said, 'Mr. Tam, that was the most decisive moment of my life.'"

Stanley Tam came back from that conversation with Lettie Cowman and told a lawyer, "I want to give my business to God."

The lawyer retorted, "That's impossible!"

"Well, then, I'll find another lawyer," Stanley said. He did just that, and the Every Creature Crusade was born.

We need that kind of sacrificial love flowing through us, the kind of love where God is central and everything else is secondary, everything else is subordinate to Him. We are living in the kingdom where God reigns and His love controls us.

God is the origin of our life. When we turn away from Him, spiritual death begins. It may take a long time, but death is inevitable.

Do you know what the Holiness Movement's message is? It is that God can be the Center of your life, so that all of your life flows from Him.

Consider for a moment what the word *obey* means. When we think of the Old Testament commands, "Thou shalt not," do we picture a legal relationship or a loving personal relationship? The Hebrew expression for "obey" is *shema laqqol*, which literally means, "listen to the voice of." There is a great difference between an attitude which says, "I've got a duty to do," and one that says, "God has said this to me, and He is my Father. He calls me His child. His only-begotten Son is wedded to me. We have a personal relationship. Shouldn't I listen to the voice of One who is related to me in such an intimate way?

The Most Important Question

As we begin a new century, the most important question I can ask you is this: *Are you listening to God?* Are you close enough to Him that you can hear what He is saying?

Another Hebrew phrase for "obey" conveys the same kind of idea. It is the word *hiqshib*, which literally means, "pay attention to." This is why Moses implored God not to send the Israelites into the wilderness unless He would be with them. They needed access to God. They needed to know He was with them. They needed Him to lead them, day by day and step by step. So they had to give God their undivided attention.

That's what Abraham did as he walked with God. He did not let anything arise in his life that would compete with God.

I started working in the Christian ministry a long time ago. Over the years, I have learned that *it's easy for the ministry to take the place of the One for whom we minister.* Yet the work of Christ will never save the world. Only Christ will save the world.

It's easy for us to get so busy in our ministry programs that we lose sight of the Lord's face and wander away from His presence. When we do, we cut our anchor line to the Source of all that is good and all that we need for life.

Father, we thank You for the gentle tug of Your Spirit that we occasionally sense from within. You speak so quietly to us. There are days when we'd like to have You shout at us, but You don't. Lord, quiet us so that we can hear Your voice, become aware of Your presence, and know that we are walking step by step with You.

Remind us that we aren't in ministry on our own. Don't let us turn away from You. Amen.

Hear what the Lord says to you, O house of Israel. This is what the Lord says:

Do not learn the ways of the nations
  or be terrified by signs in the sky,
  though the nations are terrified by them.
For the customs of the peoples are worthless;
  they cut a tree out of the forest,
  and a craftsman shapes it with his chisel.
They adorn it with silver and gold;
  they fasten it with hammer and nails
  so it will not totter.
Like a scarecrow in a melon patch,
  their idols cannot speak;
they must be carried
  because they cannot walk.
Do not fear them;
  they can do no harm
  nor can they do any good...."

I know, O Lord, that a man's life is not his own;
  it is not for man to direct his steps.

–Jeremiah 10:1-5, 23

3. Walking with God

I N the first lecture, we considered six metaphors that the Bible uses to describe our relationship with God. The first metaphor was seen in Abraham's life, the metaphor of *friendship*. Abraham had that sort of relationship with God as they walked together for so many years. We are here today because of Abraham's friendship with God. And he could not have friendship without trust.

The second metaphor was that of *legal judgment and pardon*. This metaphor first appears with the establishment of the Mosaic Law. It portrays us as standing before God, the Judge, who has found us guilty of sin and is ready to impose the sentence of death, which we deserve. But then God himself intervenes and removes the penalty, so that we are justified by faith.

The third metaphor was that of the *family*. It's an image that develops slowly in the Bible, first in Israel's relationship with God, then in terms of every believer's relationship with Him. To be a Christian is to be born a second time into the very family of God, so that we find within our hearts a spirit that cries out, "Abba, Father!"

The fourth metaphor of our relationship with God was that of *marriage*. A great deal of Scripture supports this teaching, not all of it as obvious as it might be. Scripture says that human history began with a wedding and will end with a wedding. Jesus began His public ministry with a wedding (John 2:1-11) and, in the last week before the Cross, He talked about a divine wedding that is to come (Luke 14:15-24). The theme of marriage permeates the Scriptures, culminating in the idea that we are to become the bride of Christ (Rev. 21:9-27). The human analogy that most closely resembles the relationship we are to have with Christ is the relationship we have with a person of the opposite sex, whom we love and to whom we commit ourselves irrevocably.

The fifth metaphor was *inhabitation*. Christ lives within us and we live within Christ. We dwell in Him and He dwells in us.

The sixth metaphor was *identification*. When we live and labor in Christ's name, Christ himself is there. I confess that this metaphor has troubled me the most and has forced me to come to grips with the meaning of the Atonement for my own life. If it is true that, wherever I am, Christ himself is present, then He must do something in my life far more than simply take away the penalty of my sins. He must make me in some way an image of himself. He must transform me into a kind of channel through which He can come into my world.

I think all of these metaphors emphasize the importance of the Cross. They indicate that Christ died on the cross to make possible the fulfillment of these relationships—or rather, this relationship. We do not have multiple relationships with God. It is one relationship, though we need several metaphors to describe it.

Sin and Repentance

In the second lecture, we considered the nature of sin. We said that the sin of Adam and Eve was simply that they turned away from the Lord who was the Source of all good. It is significant that the Hebrew word for "repent" literally means "to turn." This indicates we must do the opposite of what we and our ancestors have done in the past. We turned away from God; now we must turn back to Him. The Old Testament concept of repentance is simply that of restoring a relationship with God, so that we can again know the things we need from Him, the things without which we cannot live, the grace and goodness that are found only in Him. We need the Holy Spirit to help us turn to Him, so that the fullness of God's grace can enter our lives.

The ultimate end of redemption is best depicted, not by a legal image, but by a family image in which we are reunited with the heavenly Father and with His Son, so that we can call God our Father once again.

It is significant that the culmination of redemption is expressed by this family metaphor. I believe this reflects a wisdom found only in the Scriptures.

Since we have five children, sixteen grandchildren, and four great-grandchildren, I know a little about the burden of being a parent. In my early days as a father, I thought that the Ten Commandments said, "Children, obey your parents." But one day, I noticed that the passage actually says, "*Honor* your father and your mother . . ." (Ex. 20:12, emphasis mine). There is a great difference between obeying someone and honoring someone.

It is possible that someday, in order to honor my human parent, I must disobey him. But I will honor him in that disobedience. In the way that I disobey, my honoring will be evident.

E. Stanley Jones came to Asbury College, heard the message of missions, and began leading a Student Volunteer group. He asked God to give him one missionary out of that group of students. God answered that prayer, though not in the way Jones expected. God called E. Stanley Jones himself. So Stanley sat down and wrote to his widowed mother in New Jersey: "God has called me to be a missionary."

Immediately, his mother wrote back in great indignation. "You have made a mistake," she said. "I am a widow. I have no one to care for me. God would not do this. You are not called to the mission field. Your first responsibility is to take care of me."

E. Stanley Jones was stricken to the heart. He wrestled with the dilemma, but God would not let him off the hook. So he wrote back and said, "Mother, it is not that I love you less. It is simply that I must put Christ first. He will not release me from the call that He has placed upon my life."

Stanley's mother wrote back in a hot temper about how he was an unfaithful son. She eventually began to change her point of view, because she realized that she was placing her confidence in her son, not in God. So she asked God to forgive her. Although she had been an invalid, she got well and began to live a healthier life. In his later years, E. Stanley Jones would say, "I honored my mother on that occasion, even though I disobeyed her, because there is One higher than an earthly parent. That is the true Parent, God the Father. I had to obey Him."

I am glad I heard that story, because one day I had to deal with my own son, who was in a spirit of rebellion. Something deep in my spirit said, *If you insist on having your way in this, you will lose him. You may lose him forever.* For the first time, I capitulated to my son's wishes. I did not try to impose my will and my standards upon him. At the close of that conversation, he said, "Well, Daddy, do not give up on me."

When I turned my son loose, he was free to turn back to me. A willing relationship was again possible. I judged him to be wrong, but I did not abandon him. So it was still possible to maintain the kind of relationship we needed to have.

God Allows Us to Reject Him

Likewise, God is not like a dictator who stands over us, hammering away at our rebellious human will and saying, "You must obey Me!" Instead, He gives us freedom. He allows us to reject Him. Certainly, we lose much when we do that. But when we have lost, we still have a chance to come back to Him. By coming back, we can build a relationship of deep, devout love.

This is the kind of God we worship. What a great thing it is to know that, behind all the perplexing processes of the universe, there is our Father. When the early Christians formally declared their belief in God, the first thing they said was, "I believe in the Father." Examine 1 Corinthians

15:24-28. It says that when every knee has bowed and every tongue has confessed that Jesus Christ is Lord to the glory of God the Father, then the Son will render up the Kingdom to the Father from whence it came. So God is eternally our Father. He was our Father before the universe began and He will be Father in the end. We can have this kind of relationship with Him in the present. He is a personal, loving, trustworthy Father.

Every Christian wants to know the answers to two questions. First, *What is God's will for me?* In other words, *What was I made to be?* I know there is a proper destiny, a proper character, and a proper way of life for me. I need to know what God intends for me, so that I can allow Him to help me fulfil it.

Second, *What is God like?* Scripture teaches that, from the beginning, God made us human beings in His own image. He made me individually to be like himself. I need to know what He is like, so that I can allow Him to make me more like the kind of Person He is.

How can we know what God is like? We find some clear answers in Jeremiah 10:1-5. I don't believe I have heard anyone preach on this passage, yet I have lived with it for a long time and the longer I live with it, the more beautiful it becomes to me. So let me share with you the path of thinking in which it has led me.

The Nature of God

First, notice that Jeremiah is condemning idolatry. He begins the chapter by saying,

Hear what the Lord says to you, O house of Israel. This is what the Lord says:
    "Do not learn the ways of the nations or be terrified by signs in the sky, though the nations are terrified by them.
For the customs of the peoples are worthless;
    they cut a tree out of the forest, and a craftsman shapes it with his chisel.

They adorn it with silver and gold;
they fasten it with hammer and nails
so it will not totter.
Like a scarecrow in a melon patch, their
idols cannot speak;
they must be carried because they
cannot walk.
Do not fear them;
they can do no harm nor can they do
any good."

He is talking about the pagan people who live around Israel, but not only about them. He is also talking about many people who are in the community of Israel or Judah itself, because idolatry had become a religious pattern for many of the Jews. He is speaking to people who might be counted among the people of God, yet they worship and serve idols.

Notice that Jeremiah cannot conceive of someone who does not believe in a spiritual reality. That is beyond Jeremiah's comprehension. One must be influenced by modernity to think that is even possible. But in Jeremiah's world, if you did not know the true God, you would make one to take His place. Jeremiah speaks of a people whose life was filled with substitutes for the true God from whom they had turned, the God whom they no longer knew.

Jeremiah says these people are religious because mankind is innately religious. Human history gives ample evidence of that. We are sometimes ridiculously religious, and that is what Jeremiah criticizes here. He says, "You must have a god. You need someone to worship. You long to know someone who transcends your human problems. So what do you do? You go out into the woods, cut down a tree, and carve a god from it."

A god is supposed to have worth, so these people plate their idols with gold. They do not realize that they themselves attributed this value to their gods. They assume that a god is reliable and will bring stability to their lives, so they nail their image to a platform to keep it from toppling over. Since a god is supposed to be easily available, they put wheels on the platform so they can move it around, making the idol available to worship anywhere.

Jeremiah makes fun of these idol worshipers who turn away from the true God to gods of their own creation. But what does Jeremiah say about the God whom he represents? He says there is no other god like Him. Why? Because He is the only God that exists. Verses 6 and 7 say that He is the true God; the others are false. He is the living God; the others have no life at all.

Verse 12 says, "God made the earth by his power." He made everything that exists. The person sitting next to you, the seat on which you sit, the air that you breathe, everything in your life— God made it all. He is the Creator. He is the One who provides all your needs.

In verses 12-16, Jeremiah links the theme of Creation to human history. He says that God is not only the Creator who made all things, but He is the sovereign Lord of history. So God tells people of Jerusalem to pack their bags, because "at this time I will hurl out those who live in this land; I will bring distress on them so that they may be captured" (Jer. 10:18). He identifies himself as the sovereign Lord of history. He made this world and still exercises His rule in it.

The ancients knew they were made to worship Someone beyond themselves. Atheists are a modern phenomenon, and I question whether an atheist truly does not believe in God.

Even Atheists Suspect the Truth

Sam Kamaleson of World Vision graciously took me with him on a preaching mission to Moldova in 1990. While there, we visited the Ministry of Culture and Cults, the agency which waged the Communist government's persecution of the church. Three Baptist pastors accompanied us as we walked into the Ministry. I could feel the pastors' apprehension level rise.

The Minister of Culture and Cults was 6'4" tall, a movie producer, and a poet. I could tell he was a very intelligent person, yet there was an irritated tone in his voice. He seemed to be a volcano of energy, waiting to explode. Even though I did not know Russian, I could hear the annoyance in his voice. I thought, *This could be a hostile hour.*

Suddenly, he interrupted his monologue to the pastors and declared to me, "You know I am the Minister of Culture. [He did not add "Cults."] You and I both know that the way people normally express their culture is through religion. Our government has decided to take our culture away from us. The end result is, we are a people who have stared into the very face of the Devil himself, and we have come away with our flesh seared. Can you help us?"

It was an awesome moment. Here was a man who had spent his entire life in communistic atheism, yet his heart cried for something beyond himself.

Since then, I have noticed that every time I have met an outspoken atheist, I found some evidence of a belief in spiritual beings, sometimes expressed as a belief in the occult, in superstition, or in magic. All of us yearn for something beyond ourselves that we can worship. Jeremiah recognized this fact. He said that we are made for another. Will you let me capitalize that word, *Another?* We are made for Another.

Jeremiah states this conclusion in Jeremiah 10:23. I want to give you a translation of that verse which is somewhat different from the NIV. The Hebrew text is very direct at this point. It does not mince any words. It literally means:

> I know, O Yahweh, that Adam's[1] way is not in himself. It is not in the individual[2] who walks to direct his steps.

---

[1] The Hebrew word *adam* is used here to denote the entire human race.
[2] This is the Hebrew word *ish*, which signifies a particular person.

The expression "who walks" is a Hebrew participle that describes goal-orientedness. Every human being is goal-oriented. Being made in the image of God, each of us has purposes and goals. But notice again what Jeremiah says: "I know, O Yahweh, that Adam's way is not in himself. It is not in the individual who walks to direct his steps." All of us human beings want to get somewhere, but we do not know how to get there.

This is an interesting conclusion, isn't it? There must be a way for us to live, but it is not of our own making. We cannot find it on our own. So this explains why we humans are innately religious. This is the reason we cry out for Another beyond ourselves. I believe there is abundant evidence right here today to support that conclusion.

Not one human being has a built-in compass. If you intend to travel in unfamiliar territory and you cannot see the sun, you will need a compass to find your way. Without an external point of reference, a human being will go in circles. We cannot make linear progress without looking to a stationary point outside ourselves.

Looking for a Dependable Guide

A farmer's grandson once wanted to learn how to plow. So the old man said, "Son, you've got to plow in a straight line. You've got to run these furrows side by side.

"Look at something across the field," the grandfather said. "Fix your eyes on it and plow straight toward it. Then you will get a straight furrow."

The old man left the boy to his task. He came back awhile later and found that the boy had plowed all over creation. "I told you to aim toward something," the old farmer said. "I said to pick something and plow toward it."

"I did," the boy said. "I picked that cow over there!" As the cow had moved, the boy's point of reference had moved.

That is just the way we are. We need a dependable external point of reference, because there is no directional system within us. You and I are not complete packages. We are not self-sufficient. When we turn inward, we lose our direction and end up in a state of delusion. We need an unmoving point of reference beyond ourselves.

This is why Augustine said, "Lord, You have made us for yourself and we never find rest until we find it in You."[3] A businessman put it this way, "God made a hole in me so big that nothing in the world could fill it but God himself."

Jesus Christ can fill that vacuum in the human spirit. Then we will have that all-important point of reference.

When I reached this point in my study of Jeremiah 10 some years ago, I thought, *God made me so I would need Him. Isn't He shrewd? If He had not done this, I would try to live my own life and would destroy myself.*

Then I thought, *That must be the difference between the Creator and His creature. The creature needs the Creator, because the Creator made him that way.*

However, I do not believe that anymore, because I am convinced that God would not manipulate us. He would not program us with certain needs, to make us respond to Him like robots at the appropriate time. No, I believe we are dependent upon Him because of the image we share with Him.

The Nature of a Person

I am convinced that to be a person is to be oriented toward someone beyond oneself. I am well aware that this may simply be my own interpretation, but let me elaborate on this thought. I am convinced that to be a person is to be incomplete. Here's why:

We are not self-originating. Everyone here started in someone else's body. Someone carried you for nine months in her womb before you were born. You did not choose to live; life was a gift that

[3]Augustine, *Confessions*, I:1.

someone else bestowed upon you. We did not origi-
nate ourselves; we originated in someone else.

We are not self-sustaining. Three times a day,
we eat. More often than that, we drink. Eighteen
times a minute, our bodies remind us that our life is
not within us, because we must inhale air. If that
supply of oxygen is cut off, our life is over. So we
cannot sustain our own lives. We are incomplete.

We are not self-explanatory. There is no such
thing as a "typical human being." Each individual
comes from two others. If an alien exploratory team
came here from some remote corner of space and
captured one of us, carrying us back to their own
planet for analysis, they still would not know much
about the human race. There must be a male to
explain every female and a female to explain every
male. Our explanation of ourselves is not within us.

Do you know what else the Gospels tell us?
We are not self-fulfilling. I am convinced that this
fact refutes the great lie that leads to sin.

Every human being thinks, *If I can just live my
way, I'll be happy.* Adam and Eve said in the Garden, "If we can just get that fruit, we will be con-
tent." We suppose that our own way will lead to
contentment. We imagine that we will find life's fulfillment in getting what we want. That is the supreme lie of all lies. Get what you want and you will
discover that it is not what you really want. You
want something more, because you were created to
find your fulfillment outside of yourself.

Jeremiah grasped these facts. He knew that we
are not self-originating. We are not self-
sustaining. We are not self-explanatory. We are not
self-fulfilling. We need another if we are to find life's
fullness. For many years, as I read Jeremiah's ridi-
cule of idolatry, I thought, *Every creature is
incomplete. The Creator doesn't have that problem.*

But then I read what Christ says in John 5:26:
"For as the Father has life in himself, so he has
granted the Son to have life in himself."

Think of that. The eternal Son of God is like me, because He did not give himself life. He can raise you and me from the dead, but His own life comes from the Father. Isn't that fascinating? He says He is not self-originating.

Further, He says that He is not self-sustaining. My umbilical cord was cut when the midwife separated me from my mother, but Christ talks about himself and His Father as if His umbilical cord has never been cut. "I tell you the truth, the Son can do nothing by himself; he can do only what he sees His Father doing, because whatever the Father does the Son also does" (John 5:19).

Christ says He is not self-explanatory, either. Read the gospel of John and see how many times Christ calls himself the Son. That is the way He identifies himself. He is not here on His own, but He was sent by the Father. We can understand what a son is only by understanding what a parent is. So Jesus Christ is not self-explanatory. He does not stand on His own.

Most significant to me is the fact that Jesus says He is not self-fulfilling. Notice: "For I have come down from heaven not to do my will but to do the will of him who sent me" (John 6:38). Forty times the gospel of John uses the word *sent*. The Greek word is sometimes *apostello* and sometimes *pempo*, but it is always translated in English by one word—*sent*. In fact, Jesus uses a magnificent phrase in the gospel of John when He refers to His Father as *ho pempas me pater*, "the sending-Me Father" (John 8:16, 18). Who anointed the Messiah? The sending-Me Father.

Slowly, it dawned on me that the main character in the gospel of John is not Jesus. The main character is the Father who sent Jesus. That shook up my understanding of Good Friday, because I always assumed the central figure of that Day was the One on the middle cross. But the reality is, the central Figure was the One whom the spectators could not see, the One who orchestrated the whole thing. The Son was there simply to fulfil His Father's will. He said He came "to do the will of him who sent me" (John 6:38; cf. John 4:34).

Remember the passages where Jesus said He would give up His life for us (Matt. 20:28; John 6:51)? Remember what he said about the Good Shepherd: "The good shepherd lays down his life for the sheep" (John 10:11)? Do you know why a shepherd normally keeps sheep? He keeps them to sell, to shear or to eat. But Jesus says He is the Good Shepherd. He is different from other shepherds. He keeps sheep so they can eat and wear Him, not so that He can eat and wear them.

And here is the most astounding fact of all: Jesus says that I am supposed to be like Him.

How can I reach the place where I am willing to release my life and let it be poured out for somebody else? How can I let my life be sacrificed for Christ's sake? That will require something more than the forgiveness of my sins. I become like Christ only when He gets me to the place where He can spend me as He will.

When we share the Lord's Supper, we hear those words, "Take and eat; this is my body.... Drink from [this cup], all of you. This is my blood of the covenant, which is poured out for many for the forgiveness of sins" (Matt. 26:26-27). Jesus is literally saying, "Consume Me. Devour Me."

And then He says most pointedly, "As the Father has sent Me, I am sending you" (John 20:21).

If we are to change the world in which we live during the twenty-first century, we must take our hands off of our own lives so that the Lord can spend us in whatever way He pleases. When that kind of spending takes place, people will ask, "How do they do that?" And then Jesus Christ is revealed.

My gifts do not accomplish Christian service. My training will not do it. My skills cannot do it.

Only self-sacrifice will make a difference in the world. Only the Cross can set me free from the sin that would hold me back. Only the atoning sacrifice of Christ can cause me to say, "Father, I want Your way, no matter what the cost. I want Your way totally because I know that anything else is deceptive and ultimately destructive. If I can just be wholly Yours, I will find out what You made me for. I will find my life's fulfillment, because that fulfillment is not in myself. It is in another—maybe in the life of someone I would not choose, but in someone else and for purposes eternal. That is the only way I can truly be alive."

I think this is what the Cross is all about.

Our Father, we misunderstood Your Son when He came because He was so different from what we expected. We knew we should kneel before the One we worship. Then You sent us the eternal Son of God, who knelt at our feet. We knew that sacrifice was a fitting part of worship. Then we came to Calvary, where the One we worshiped gave himself as the sacrifice for us.

O God, You have a way of turning everything upside down. So we often misunderstand You. Quicken our minds, quicken our hearts, quicken our understanding so that we can see what kind of Person You really are. Teach us to trust You enough to let You do whatever You will with us. Amen.

Be imitators of God, therefore, as dearly loved children and live a life of love, just as Christ loved us and gave himself up for us as a fragrant offering and sacrifice to God.

—Ephesians 5:1-2

4. Being Imitators of God

ALTHOUGH I am nearly eighty years old, I still am amazed at how many things I find in the Bible that I never have seen before, things that appear in unexpected places. Perhaps they are things that I have deliberately skipped over. But in some way or other, the Holy Spirit now brings them into focus for me and they come alive.

I recently decided to read the epistle to the Ephesians from beginning to end. So I blocked out some time, sat down alone, and started. Eventually, I found myself reading chapter five, which Paul begins by saying, "Be imitators of God, therefore, as dearly loved children" (Eph. 5:1). I laughed out loud and thought, *Paul, you have really missed it. How could I ever be an imitator of God?*

God is the Omnipotent One. Granted, a few people in human history have tried to play God's role. They have attempted to control everything, but each of them has proven to be a fool. A human being certainly cannot imitate God's omnipotence.

God is the Omniscient One. He knows everything. We cannot inform Him of anything. There are no surprises for Him. I am the exact opposite. If I have a question and pursue it long enough, I may be able to find an answer; but in the process, I realize there are ten things more which I do not know. A human being seems to have limitless ignorance, not limitless knowledge. So how can any human be an imitator of God's omniscience?

Moreover, God is the Omnipresent One. He is everywhere at once. By contrast, I am located at one moment in time and one spot in space, and there is no way I can break out of that. How under the sun can a human being imitate the omnipresent God?

Then I took a second look at the Scripture passage and realized that Paul defines specifically what He means when he says that we are to imitate God: "And walk in love, as Christ also hath loved us, and hath given himself for us as an offering and a sacrifice to God for a sweet-smelling savour" (Eph. 5:2, KJV).

Paul says we should walk in love, as Christ does. Here we again encounter the word for *walk*, which we said was the key word for the book of Genesis. Our models of faith in the book of Genesis are people who walked with God. They were His friends. So God moves Paul to write in this Ephesian letter, "I want you to be like those who have walked with Me."

Walking is not a single act. Paul must not be exhorting us to do one specific thing. He is talking about a pattern that should characterize our lives. He describes a relationship that is abiding, continuing, and determinative in our existence, so that our actions come out of the pattern of our lives. That pattern is one of unbroken communion with God. That communion with Him determines how we act and think.

I am grateful for Scripture's emphasis upon my life pattern rather than my acts, because there may be moments when I look the other way or when I slip from being in an intimate partnership with God. Occasionally, something shows up in my life that really does not fit the pattern of Christlike living. Then He checks me and brings me back to himself.

So I say, "Lord, I want Your life to be the pattern for me. I want Your way of living to be my norm for living, not the exception." This is what Paul means when he says, "Walk in love, even as Christ also hath loved us, and hath given himself for us" (Eph. 5:2, KJV).

The Greek word *agapé* ("love") appears in this verse. One cannot find the meaning of "self-giving love" applied to this word in Greek etymological dictionaries or in the secular Greek literature, because this concept was foreign to the ancient Greek mind. But the New Testament uses *agapé* to denote a love in which a person cares more about others than he cares about himself. It is more than loving your neighbor as yourself; it is loving your neighbor so much that you sacrifice yourself for that neighbor. It is a love in which the well-being of others is more important to you than your own well-being. So when the Apostle Paul describes how we are to "walk," he says we should walk in that kind of love. Christ is our pattern for living.

You know, when we American Christians read the life of Christ and we are reminded of His miracles, we desire to see such miraculous things in our own day. We have a great interest in the miraculous. Yet behind those miracles, we find Christ's expression of His own purpose when He says, "Not as I will, but as you will" (Matt. 26:39).

The apostle Paul says, "Walk in love, even as Christ also hath loved us, and hath given himself for us." That word, *give*, has important religious overtones in the Greek language, because it is often found in ritual writings. A person who makes a sacrifice is said to be *giving* it to his god. The apostle says that is what Christ did. He gave himself to the Father in sacrifice for us. Therefore, Paul says, we should give ourselves likewise in sacrifice for others.

Ephesians 5:2 is full of Greek words with specialized religious meanings. Take the word for *offering*, for example. It's the Greek word, *prosphora*, which is equivalent to the Old Testament's *mincha*, a word broadly used to describe gifts given to God. The second word Paul uses for "offering," *thusian*, is the New Testament equivalent of the Old Testament's *zabach*. From that word comes the Hebrew word for "altar," *mizbeach*. So the "offering" is often slaughtered. Something dies in the process of making an offering to God. Something ends its existence because it is given to One who will use it for other purposes. Paul is saying your "walk"—i.e., your life—should be a sacrificial one, in which you give yourself to others in the same way that Christ gave himself for us.

The shadow that falls over all of this language is Golgotha, the place of the Cross. There Christ sacrificed himself on our behalf. Remember, God wants us to be like Christ. So He expects us to offer ourselves sacrificially for the sake of others.

In the Garden, Adam and Eve fell into a lie because the serpent said, "Your eyes will be opened, and you will be like God, knowing good and evil" (Gen. 3:5). I believe they immediately thought, *God is in control around here. The snake says that if we eat this fruit, we will become like God. So then we will be in control.*

That was the first lie perpetrated upon the human mind. The God who put His children in the Garden was not obsessed with controlling them. He had said, "It is all yours. Just stay away from that particular kind of fruit, because you will lose your connection with good if you partake of that. You will come to know what evil is" (cf. Gen. 2:15-17). Now, what kind of God is that? Is that a controlling, manipulating God?

Four Figures of Christ

Four figures of Christ in the gospel of John further dispel that notion about the character of God. The first figure we have of Christ is that He came abjectly. "Even in his own land and among his own people, he was not accepted" (John 1:11, NLT). Jesus did not come with great worldly glory and power, the way the Jews expected their Messiah to come. He came almost plaintively knocking at the door of their world and saying, "Will you let Me in?" That is not the attitude of a manipulator, is it? The one knocking is not in control of the situation; the person on the other side of the door is in control. In Christ, we see the greatest picture of God that we can find. What did Christ do? He knocked at the door of our world and said, "You have the control over this relationship. I will not coerce or manipulate you. I just want you to use your control in the right way."

A father can understand this. A husband can understand this. A wife can understand this. None of us wants to dominate a family member whom we really love. At the same time, we don't want to be controlled by those around us. The amazing thing is that the eternal God does not try to control our lives. A compulsory relationship is not what He wants with us, and it is not the kind of relationship He invites us to have with Him. He asks us to do His will because we delight in doing it. If we enjoy pleasing Him, then His will becomes our will.

The second image of Christ in the gospel of John is that He came humbly. He did not ride into Jerusalem on a horse, but on a donkey (Matt. 21:1-5). In the ancient world, the horse was a military animal, while the donkey was a servant's beast. I suppose I had read the Bible for fifty years before I saw the real significance of Zechariah 9:9–10, which says,

> See, your king comes to you,
>   righteous and having salvation,
>   gentle and riding on a donkey,
>   on a colt, the foal of a donkey.
> I will take away the chariots from Ephraim
>   and the war-horses from Jerusalem,
>   and the battle-bow will be broken.

Christ is not a horse king. He is a donkey King. When I realized this in the 1980s, a good deal of Arab money was flowing into Kentucky to buy race horses. Fifteen miles from my home, auctioneers sold a horse that had never run a step in a race—

a yearling—for $10.5 million dollars. So I asked someone what the going rate for donkeys was at Lexington. I was told that I could buy a good donkey for about sixty-five dollars. I saw theology in that fact. Because Jesus Christ was not a horse king, the Jewish leaders said, "We don't know what to do with this fellow. He doesn't fit our expectations."

Another figure of Christ is seen on Maundy Thursday at the Upper Room. What is Christ doing there? He gets down on His knees before His disciples (John 13:2-5).

Kneeling is a religious act. There's nothing more pious than to kneel before the One you worship—kneel before the One whose blessing you seek. Anywhere you find religious people, they will kneel sooner or later. They may even prostrate themselves before the One whom they worship.

But here, as never before in human history, the One who is worshiped kneels before the worshiper. Suddenly, the religious practices of the ages are turned upside-down. Who is on His knees? The eternal God. That is the God we are supposed to resemble, the God we are supposed to imitate. He indeed wants us to be just like Him—not so that he can humiliate us, but so that He can make us all that we can be for His sake.

The final figure of Christ in the gospel of John appears on Good Friday (John 19:16-18). Without question, the Cross was an altar and on it hung a Sacrifice. You cannot have religion without a sacrifice. What is sacrifice? It is something valuable which the worshiper gives to the worshiped. For millennia of religious history, a common characteristic of worship has been that a worshiper will recognize the worshiped with a sacrifice.

But what do we have on Good Friday? We have the eternal God giving His greatest possession—His own Son—as a sacrifice for those who worship Him. The whole picture is upside-down.

So when Ephesians 5:1 says, "Be imitators of God," our first impulse is to think the way Adam and Eve did, when they imagined God as the Sovereign Controller of the world. But Paul says we should get our thinking straight. When he tells us to imitate God, he means we must love others as He loved us and gave himself for us.

Imitate God, Who Was Willing to Die

I am convinced that we have misunderstood the very character of God, particularly in terms of His self-sacrifice and willingness to die. When we think of total surrender, we suppose it is a sort of ignominious thing in which we capitulate to someone else. That is a false image. Surrender is the way of deliverance and freedom. God lets us go through what appears to be the ignominy of surrender, bowing the knee and all the rest; but in doing so, He is freeing us from that which contaminates our lives so that we can stand clean, as children of God should be able to stand before Him.

As I was thinking about this matter of self-sacrifice, I remembered another sermon by Henry Clay Morrison. It was a sermon on Abraham's sacrifice of Isaac. God said to Abraham, "Take your son, your only son, Isaac, whom you love, and go to the region of Moriah. Sacrifice him there as a burnt offering..." (Gen. 22:2).[1]

Morrison said, "When Abraham lifted that knife and was ready to put it into the person he loved the most—his life, his joy, his pride, his hope—only then did he hear a voice that said, 'Don't touch the lad.'

---

[1] An astounding line occurs in this story when God says, "Take your son and sacrifice him." The next word in the Hebrew text is *vayashkem*, meaning, "He arose early" (Gen. 22:3). So the first thing the next morning, Abraham went to do what his Friend had told him to do—to sacrifice the object of his love. He went out to sacrifice his future and his very reason for existence. So Abraham had plenty of reason to argue with God if he wanted, but... *Vayashkem* ("He arose early.")

"At that point, I think I heard another conversation," Morrison said. "It was a conversation between the eternal Father and the eternal Son. The Son said, 'Father this is not the last time we are coming to this mountaintop, is it?'

"And the Father said, 'No, Son. In about two thousand years, we will come back here.'

"'And, Father, the next time we come to this mountaintop, it will not be one of them on the altar. It will be one of Us, won't it?'

"And the eternal Father said, 'Yes, Son. The next time we come back, one of Us will be on the altar.'

"'I will be the One, won't I?' the Son asked.

"And the Father said, 'That's right.'

"'Father, when they are ready to put the nails into my hands and the spear into my side, are You going to cry out, "Don't touch the lad!?"'

"'No, Son,' the Father said. 'We never ask them to do in symbol what we have not done in reality.'"

God will reign, but not as the manipulative kind of ruler who wants us under His power so He can extort from us whatever pleases Him. He is a Father who wants His children to grow and become all that they can be. He is a Spouse who wants His companion to grow and blossom into full maturity.

Paul says that when we care more about someone else than we do about ourselves, we become "a sweet-smelling savour to God" (Eph. 5:2, KJV). That idea intrigues me. You and I buy plenty of deodorant so no one will ever be able to smell our offensive body odor. God says, "If you will become a living sacrifice for Me, in the same way that I became one for you, then you will be a glorious aroma to My nostrils."

The English translation of this verse uses the words "sweet-smelling savour." Behind that phrase are two Greek words, *osmein* and *euodias*.

These words are the Greek translation of two Hebrew words which are used consistently throughout the sacrificial literature of the Old Testament—*reach nichoach*. The phrase suggests that any sacrifice made to God becomes a sweet-smelling and pleasing fragrance to His nostrils.

Several years ago, I pulled down the *Encyclopedia Britannica* to read the article on frankincense, and I discovered that frankincense comes from a tree. Do you know how the fragrance is extracted from that tree? The plantation workers slash it. They take sharp, heavy knives or hatchets and slash the bark of the tree, then cut away the bark below the wound, and wait while the tree bleeds its sap. The encyclopedia used an unfamiliar word to describe the drops of sap, saying that they are expelled in *ovate* form. The word *ovate* primarily means "egg-shaped," but it also means "tear-shaped." So the tree weeps its sap. Then the sap is left to harden. When it has hardened, the pieces are crushed, ground to powder, and dissolved in a solvent. Only when the tree loses its own life fluid can it make the world a better-smelling place.

As Christians, our lives are like that. We are supposed to be a sweet-smelling savor in the nostrils of God, but we can accomplish that only by surrendering our own lives for His sake.

Paul is not giving a call to repentance in Ephesians 5. He is not talking here about putting away deliberate, conscious transgressions. He is talking about the self-interest that tries to protect what the individual holds dear. So Paul's appeal is not addressed to unbelievers. He issues the call to holiness to believers, because a person must be a believer before one can learn how deep-seated the sinfulness is inside one's own heart. Paul is not speaking to people who need to break a pattern of sinful living. He is speaking to people who have already done that. He is saying, "I want

The Call to Abandon Self-Interest

you to know something deeper. The Cross brought you forgiveness, but the Cross also can bring you deliverance from the contamination of self-interest."

That contamination runs deep—so deep that God must take it into account when He calls us to himself. When Adam and Eve sinned (i.e., when human beings first turned away from God), all of our priorities were turned inward instead of outward. And since we turned inward, the only appeal that makes any sense to us is an appeal to our own self-interest. So God must appeal to our sinful motives in order to save us.

We evangelicals often say, "God has a wonderful plan for your life."

An unbeliever asks, "Is it better than what I'm doing now? If it's better than what I'm doing now, I would like it." That is self-interest, isn't it?

Or we say, "You can have your guilt taken away."

An unbeliever responds, "You mean I do not have to live with the emotional burden of guilt? I can have that rolled away?"

"Yes," we say. We appeal to the unbeliever's self-interest.

The center of this dialogue is the self. God can appeal to nothing else in lost human beings but their sinful self-interest.

A husband and wife who are having trouble in their marriage say, "Can Christ help us?" They become Christians to save their relationship.

Someone else faces imminent death and is afraid of God's judgment. So he surrenders his life to Christ to avoid damnation.

You see, God seldom confronts us with the true depth of our self-interest at the time of our conversion, because we do not know how deep it runs. I am sure God could do anything He wanted, but normally a person cannot experience God's forgiveness of sin until he knows that he is a sinner.

If an unbeliever does not yet know the depths of his own self-interest, how can he call on God to set him free from it?

Therefore, Paul can only invite believers to give up their identities in order that the world may know Christ. He does not call unbelievers to do this.

When sin entered our world, it intensified some things and deadened others. One of the things it intensified was our ability to see what was wrong in other people. One of the things it deadened was our ability to see what is wrong with ourselves. We have a knack for seeing what is inappropriate in another person but a blindness to the same thing in ourselves.

So every human being needs two things. First, we need Christ. We need to see Him as He really is. We need to see the Holy One, who lives lovingly for someone beyond himself. Second, we need to have some people around us who can see where we do not fit Christ's pattern.

The Gospels illustrate this. When Jesus brought the disciples to Caesarea Philippi, He asked who they thought He was. Peter said, "You are the Christ, the Son of the living God" (Matt. 16:16). Jesus affirmed that this was true. He then wanted the disciples to realize who they were, so he began talking to them about going to the Cross. Luke says, "The disciples did not understand any of this. Its meaning was hidden from them, and they did not know what he was talking about" (Luke 18:34).

They knew Jesus was headed for Jerusalem. They knew that Jerusalem was the capital city of the Jews, the Passover was approaching, and Jesus was the Messiah. So they began to wonder, *Might He establish His kingdom on this trip? If He does, what will that mean for us?*

James and John asked if they could sit on Jesus' right and left when He would be enthroned. The other ten disciples became very angry when they heard this (Mark 10:35-41). They probably thought, *Who do these fellows think they are, that they should have the right hand and the left hand in the Kingdom? Who are we?* The disciples wanted to know their position.

This desire for recognition and status is a persistent problem among believers. It was among the Twelve, and it is in most of the Christian circles in which I move today.

The Ability to See Others' Potential

When God came in fullness to his heart, William Booth realized that nobody was beyond sacred potential. Harold Begbie's book, *Twice Born Men*, tells how General Booth's adjutant passed an alley one night in a storm and noticed a bundle of rags lying there. She thought, *Could there be someone beneath that pile?* So she stopped and pulled the rags away. There she found a drunken man who was dying because of the cold. She took him and cared for him. The man became known as O.B.D. ("Old Born Drunk") because his mother was drunken when he was delivered, so he had had alcohol in his system from the day of his birth. He had no memory of ever being without alcohol until Christ came into his life. He then became one of the great soul winners in Booth's Salvation Army in London.

You see, nobody is beyond the reach of God's grace. Yet that is not the way we normally think, nor did Jesus' disciples. This is why James and John said of the Samaritans, "Lord, do you want us to call fire down from heaven to destroy them?" (Luke 9:54). They could not imagine that God could do anything with those heathen people.

One of the greatest American preachers of the twentieth century was Harold John Ockenga. He was a student in a Christian college group when he said something inappropriate, and another boy in the quartet observed, "Ockie, either there is something wrong with you or there is something wrong with me." That shook Ockenga. He prayed like fury over that incident and repented of what he had done. A few weeks later, a second lapse occurred. Another person in the quartet said, "Ockie, there must be something wrong with you, or else there is something wrong with me." Out of that came an experience that Ockenga later called his total surrender, his absolute commitment to God, and the baptism of the Holy Spirit.

Dr. Ockenga invited Billy Graham to New England shortly after the Los Angeles crusade. Billy walked into the office and said to the secretary, "Could I see Dr. Ockenga?"

She replied, "Oh, I'm sure he would be delighted to see you. He is in his office. Go right on in."

When Billy went inside, he saw nobody behind the desk. Then he heard an agonizing moan, the cry of someone in great anguish of soul. He thought, *Someone is in need. Where is he?*

Behind the desk, he finally noticed that the carpet had a lump under it. When Mr. Graham pulled it up, he found Harold John Ockenga underneath the rug, praying.

I do not know whether you or I are supposed to do that sort of thing, but I will tell you this: The Spirit of God is not Someone I can use for my ministry. He is entitled to use me. And when I want to be used by the Spirit, my heart cries for Him.

I say again that the call to holiness cannot be given to sinners. The most anguished expressions in Scripture are not addressed to the world in general. They are not delivered to Rome or Alexandria or Athens. They come to Jerusalem. The great calls of the Old Testament are made to the people of God, because God says, "If *my* people, who are called by *my* name, will humble themselves and pray..." (2 Chron. 7:14, italics added).

The greatest need in the world today is not for evangelism. From my perspective, the greatest need is for Christians like you and me to be spiritually cleansed so that the Spirit of God can

What the World Needs from Us

work through us. Only when God got 120 Christians filled with the Holy Spirit could 3,000 people be converted (Acts 1:15; 2:41). Evangelism must grow out of the holiness experience. That is what happened to General William Booth and so many others who have won the lost to Christ.

As Paul writes the epistle to the Philippians, he is in prison, writing to some people whom he loves deeply. He says, "Now I want you to know, brothers, that what has happened to me has really served to advance the gospel. As a result, it has become clear throughout the whole palace guard and to everyone else that I am in chains for Christ. Because of my chains, most of the brothers in the Lord have been encouraged to speak the word of God more courageously and fearlessly" (Phil. 1:12-14).

Then we come to an appalling verse: "Some indeed preach Christ even of envy and strife; and some also of good will" (Phil. 1:15, KJV). The word translated here as "strife" does not literally mean strife. Our Greek scholars missed this for years. The word is *erithea*, and scholars thought it came from the Greek word *eridzo*, which means "to strive." In fact, this word is derived from another linguistic root. Originally, it referred to a gift of appreciation given to someone else. Then it came to refer to an earned wage. The next use of the word referred to a bribe given to a political figure. Finally, it was used of a harlot's pay. So the word basically means a payment made to advance a person's own interests.

Now notice the context in which Paul writes these words. He is in prison, shackled with chains. He knows there are a lot of people in the streets, preaching the gospel. Some of them preach out of good will, while some preach the gospel to advance themselves in some way. So he concludes, "Do nothing out of selfish ambition [*erithea*] or vain conceit, but...your attitude should be the same as that of Christ Jesus" (Phil. 2:3, 5). The *erithea* mind-set asks, "What's in it for me? What will I get out of this?" The mind-set of Christ says, "I have an opportunity to pour out my life for someone else."

So how does a person arrive at this point? Only through a divine operation of grace, done in our hearts by the Holy Spirit. The same Spirit who moved in Christ must turn us inside-out, cleansing us from the desire to keep a finger of control on our lives for personal advantage. He alone can deliver us from the inner voice constantly saying, *What will make me look good? What's in it for me? I deserve better than this.*

In four of the five other biblical references to *erithea,*[2] this way of thinking is closely related to envy—the nagging concern that others are getting more than oneself. It is the very opposite of the way Christ thought. The word *erithea* also occurs twice (2 Cor. 12:20 and Gal. 5:20) in catalogs of evil that are the opposite of the Spirit-filled life.

Is it really possible to live free of such self-interested thinking in this world? Is it possible to be delivered from the tyranny of self? Not many people believe that it is.

I have a friend who is as good a systematic theologian as I have ever met. I have read his writings and learned much from them. He says, "You know, I am an Augustinian. I do not believe it is possible to be saved from self-interest. It will contaminate everything you do."

But then he says, "I am enamored with the Wesleyan revival. I am a child of George Whitefield and not of the Wesleys, yet I have to admit that the Methodist movement came closer to producing a Christian ethos than any other movement in the history of the church. I only wish that

[2] 2 Corinthians 12:20; Galatians 5:20; James 3:14, 16; and Romans 2:8.

Wesleyans today had more of what Wesley had." He cannot stomach Wesley's theology, but he surely likes the fruit that came from it.

I am not interested in peddling John Wesley, either. It is the message of Jesus Christ that I want to "peddle." So I think we can confidently tell the world that it is possible for God, through the shed blood of Christ, to give us a clean heart. Moreover, we need to live in close communion with other Christians so that we do not deceive ourselves into complacency.

Any Examples of Selfless Servants?

We find scriptural evidence of people who were delivered from the self-centered mind. Paul says in Philippians 2:19-21, "I hope in the Lord Jesus to send Timothy to you soon, that I also may be cheered when I receive news about you. I have no one else like him, who takes a genuine interest in your welfare. For everyone looks out for his own interests, not those of Jesus Christ."

Perhaps there were not a great many people in Paul's day who sincerely cared for others and not for themselves, but Paul says that Timothy was one. How did Timothy get to that point? Was he just more virtuous than other people? No, that would be a complete contradiction of biblical theology. Timothy must have gotten to that point by the grace of Christ. And if Timothy could get there by the grace of Christ, so can you and I. We fail to get there only if we do not take advantage of the grace of Christ offered to us.

We are often reminded that Paul said he was the worst of sinners (1 Tim. 1:15), but do you know what else he said? "Do not cause anyone to stumble, whether Jews, Greeks or the church of God—even as I try to please everybody in every way. For I am not seeking my own good, but the good of many, so that they may be saved. Follow my example, as I follow the example of Christ" (1 Cor. 10:32-11:1).

Eight verses earlier, Paul had said, "Nobody should seek his own good, but the good of others" (1 Cor. 10:24). Can God indeed turn someone inside-out like that? Can He turn Luther's "incurved heart" outward? I think He can. But He will do it only when we are willing to say, "Father, not my will, but Thine be done."

The amazing thing is, when God controls your life, you are truly free. You are freer than ever before. You experience a joy that you could not know before, because you are now all that God made you to be—a reflection of Him.

Father, we can take no credit for anything we know today. All that we know and all that we have experienced have come to us because someone else cared for us. We marvel at the way You have made us, so that the key to each person's life must be found in someone else. Truly, none of us can glory in ourselves. If we know anything about Your grace today, it is because someone else paid the price to make it known to us.

Lord, let us be willing to pay the price so that others can know as much as we know—perhaps even more. Let us not be afraid to let a God who died on a cross take control of our lives. Only when You are in control can we become fully free. Amen.

Index of Scripture References